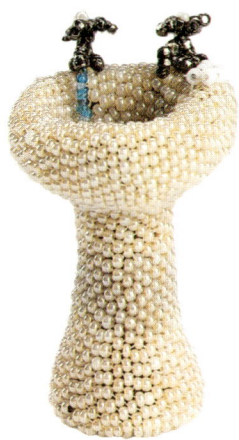

Beadwork I: Up Close

Editor, Jean Campbell
Production Editor, Mona Pompili
Production Coordinator, Nancy Disney
Production, Dean Howes, Elizabeth R. Mrofka
Photography, Joe Coca
Text copyright © 1998, Interweave Press, Inc.

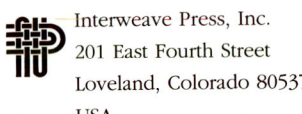 Interweave Press, Inc.
201 East Fourth Street
Loveland, Colorado 80537
USA

Printed in the United States of America

Beadwork I: Up Close

ISBN 1-883010-64-0

First Printing: IWP—3M:1198:KP

Beadwork I: Up Close

Tour

Loveland Museum, Loveland, Colorado
November 20–December 20, 1998

Textile Arts Centre, Chicago, Illinois
January 15–February 28, 1999

West Valley Art Museum, Phoenix, Arizona
May 3–June 18, 1999

Contemporary Crafts Museum, Portland, Oregon
July 1–9, 1999

American Craft Museum in conjunction with
the Bead Society of Greater New York's annual event
July 24–25, 1999

All tour dates are subject to change.

This exhibit is also available as a slide show. Contact Interweave Press at (800) 272-2193 for more information.

Beadwork I: Up Close

Jean Campbell, Editor, Beadwork

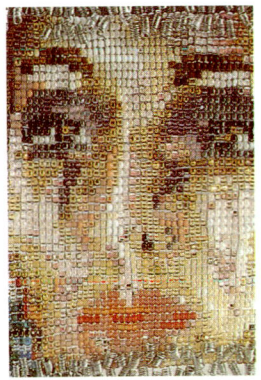

Excitement about the show was high throughout the building, and the whole staff was swept up in the enthusiasm.

From conception to opening night, Beadwork I: Up Close has been a great experience for us at Interweave Press. For me, the exhibit has been like tending a garden—I've enjoyed nurturing it, watching it grow, and seeing it come to fruition.

Starting out, I wasn't sure how many entries our call would bring, but advertising in *Beadwork* and at shops around the country elicited a huge response. When those first entries arrived, I knew we had really started something. I was overwhelmed by the quality of work from the ninety-two beadworkers who entered, and it was refreshing to see the actual pieces as opposed to slides. Being able to feel the beadwork meant so much, as did carefully examining the technique, seeing the pieces in all three dimensions.

Bonnie Hoover, Interweave's office services leader, found herself penned in behind a wall of boxes for a week as she slowly but carefully checked in the 156 pieces that came from the United States, Canada, the United Kingdom, and Argentina. Every once in a while I'd get a call from her, "Jean, Jean! You need to come see this one right away!" Excitement about the show was high throughout the building, and the whole staff was swept up in the enthusiasm. Coworkers would constantly stop by the *Beadwork* office to check the day's mail treasures.

Beadwork staffers Amy Clarke, Mona Pompili, and I laid out all the work in a large room, carefully arranging the pieces so that anonymity would be maintained. Each of us picked our favorites, but we were curious to learn what the judges' choices would be. Mimi Holmes, Connie Lehman, and Tom Lundberg came in on a Friday morning and locked themselves in the room with all the pieces. Their initial guide was the criteria we had set for the exhibit: all pieces created in the last year; a diameter of no more than 4" × 4" × 4"; and the surface covered with at least fifty percent beads. Beyond the formal guidelines, the decisions were left to the judges' academic, artistic, intuitive, and technical expertise.

Whenever I popped my head in during the day, I could see that pieces formerly left "out" had been put back "in" and vice versa. Mimi, Connie, and Tom agonized and argued over their choices. Occasionally they'd ask Amy to search out an artist's statement to further study a certain piece. Finally they came to a point of compromise and chose 46 pieces.

Overall, the sensitivity that the judges employed amazed me. They got right to the heart of each piece, and their choices reflect their insights. After the judging they felt it was important to spend lots of time writing comments about the work that didn't make the final cut. This was a tough job—after spending so much time with the pieces and becoming attached to many, I was thankful I wasn't on the jury.

Our first exhibit elicits wonder, amazement, amusement, and inspiration—a pretty incredible feat when you consider that each piece is sized no larger than your fist. If you get to see the show in person, bring you magnifying glass to enjoy it "up close." In the meantime, I hope these photographs help you treasure this little garden of beaded delights as much as I do.

The Jurors

Mimi Holmes

One Last Desire
Beads and sequins   3⅓" × 4" × 7½"

I was captivated by works that truly dealt with the Up Close theme and which I suspect were made specifically for the exhibition. Most haunting are the ones that leave me with questions: Who will use this tiny chessboard and sink? Could I follow the directions on the visual map pieces? How did the artist create the surface on the exterior of this geode? Works that call me back to them, works that I can't figure out in a single viewing, are art well worth contemplating again and again. My hope as a juror is that a number of these beaded works will stay in your mind long after you've left the show.

Mimi Holmes is a nationally known artist who has worked with beads for over fifteen years. She has shown her work in over 200 exhibitions in thirty-eight states and has juried seven exhibitions, including *Bead Dreams; Future Visions; Invitational Bead Expo; Seed Dreams, Beaded Visions;* and *Fiberarts '92.*

Connie Lehman

Lifeboat: Queen & Leta
Beads and thread   5⅜" × 6¼"

I applaud the forty-six artists who were challenged to create so many interesting, clever, artistic small wonders. Beads are already so beautiful and seductive that to use them to create one's own image is a grand achievement.

Connie Lehman is a studio artist specializing in beads, fibers, and metal. A beadworker for the last fifteen years, she has participated in over twenty-five artist-in-residencies including several underwritten by the National Endowment for the Arts. Connie has been featured in all five books published by FiberArts, and recently exhibited her work in Seattle's *Muse of the Millenium*.

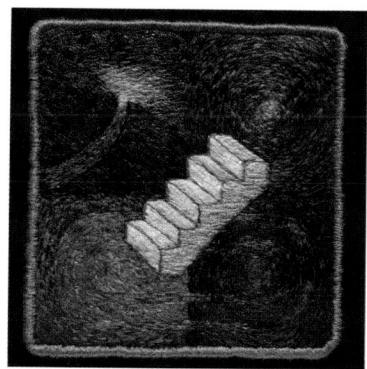

Tom Lundberg

Five Steps
Cotton and silk threads on cotton   3" × 3⅛"

Congratulations to the artists whose works were selected for this exhibit. Their creations exhibit what the jurors considered to be the best blending of concept, design, and technique to convey personal vision and fresh points of view. Kudos to Interweave Press for nurturing the growth of this medium.

Tom Lundberg is Professor of Art at Colorado State University, where he coordinates the program in fibers. His small scale embroideries are exhibited internationally and are in collections such as the American Craft Museum and the Indianapolis Museum of Art.

Tapestry #5
Delica beads   3⅞" × 3¾"
Barbara Aubrey   New York, New York

My designs utilize the interplay between color and bead type. The tapestries, when displayed vertically between glass, change as the light source changes—opaque beads pop out, translucent beads recede. This is the interplay that I love.

Up Close and Personal: Reach out and Touch Someone
Glass beads, rock, leather, nylon thread   4" × 4" × 1½"
Joanne Bast   Littlestown, Pennsylvania

Pictographs and petroglyphs, prevalent in aboriginal cultures all over the world, are documented more as tools of communication than expressions of art. The need to touch others with information—battles, journeys, locations of waterholes— appears to be a human necessity from the earliest times.

The shadings surrounding the human pictographic figures are inspired by the natural values in the underlying rock. The transposition into bead units of natural shadings for shadow are like the pixels of computer and television screens.

The current age of information blooming over the Internet is not so novel to human nature after all.

Sea Creature
Seed beads, mixed media, thread   4" × 3½" × 3½"
Jo Ann Baumann   Glencoe, Illinois

My need to communicate my creative vision and the magic seductive beauty of beads inspires me to create these whimsical forms. I want to express my delight in their infinite possible forms, textures, and sounds. The beads call to my soul, to be heard as well as seen.

Sea Creature II
Seed beads, mixed media, thread   4" × 4" × 3½"
Jo Ann Baumann   Glencoe, Illinois

We Carry Our Stories With Us
Cotton, linen paper, glass beads, embroidery thread   2" × 2" × ¾"
Bonnie Berkowitz   Hampton, New Jersey

I believe that art must retain the mark of the hand. Art infused into everyday life will elevate the quality of that life. I work with a range of materials; the struggle and the discoveries come from integrating imagery, color, and stories which will impact the private, the personal, and the public self.

Out of My Shell Series: Strawberry Top
Seed beads, embellished white hearts, silk thread   3¼" × 3¼" × 3"
Ingrid Bernhardt   Richmond, Virginia

Translating the emotion revealed in my craft into words can be difficult because the words have not yet surfaced. The pieces I create become the emotion and, therefore, the words.

Out of My Shell Series IV: Virginia Spiral
Seed beads, bugles, silk thread   2" × 3" × 3"
Ingrid Bernhardt   Richmond, Virginia

Trilogy: Three Nesting Boxes with Cap
Seed beads, bugles, rondelles, ponies 3¾" × 3¾" × 3¾"
Ingrid Bernhardt   Richmond, Virginia

Set of Three Perfume Bottles
Seed beads, silver beads   4" × 4" × 3½"
Theresa Biagoli   San Juan, Argentina

This set was created to use the large sterling silver beads as bottle stoppers. With my "box chain" stitch as the support for the structure of the bottles and peyote and/or brick stitches for the shaping, three very different shapes emerged.

Formal Attire
Delicas, framed Swarovski crystal, Nymo thread   2¾" × 2" × ⅞"
Bonnie Bousquet-Smith   Brunswick, Maine

When I learned right-angle weave, the beadwork was so like fabric I just had to make clothing. **Formal Attire** *was the first piece I made with this technique. After I created a "fancy blouse," a tie and a watch fob were necessary accessories.*

Wart
Delicas, Czechoslovakian glass drops, Nymo thread 2¼" × 2⅜" × 2¼"
Bonnie Bousquet-Smith Brunswick, Maine

I had been making beaded purses for about two years and wanted to create other pieces. I made some beaded baskets, then other vessels followed. **Wart** *is so named because throughout the creative process I was not sure I liked "him." Then "he" grew on me.*

Up Close 19

Self Portrait
Glass seed beads, wire   4" × 4"
Bo Breda   Smithville, Tennessee

I am interested in broken images—mosaics, knitted patterns, pointillism, and digitized images. Beadwork explores this way of seeing. I use metal warp because I can shape and distort the piece. However, the beads are strung on invisible monofilament because I do not want to change the translucence of the beads.

Mom's Mutant Cactus.
Seed beads, Indian glass beads, glass buttons, wood beads, nylon thread   4" × 4" × 3"
Marian Crane   Chandler, Arizona

Mom's Mutant Cactus *memorializes my Mom's daydream of a blue-flowered cactus.*

Up Close   21

Pocket Garden
Seed beads, carved wood, leather, waxed linen   2" × 3" × 1"
Marian Crane   Chandler, Arizona

Pocket Garden *is a book containing four beaded snapshots of a southern Colorado valley—a view from orbit, the valley itself, a cellular diagram of one leaf, and finally, a single carbon atom in its cloud of electrons.*

Reef # 2
Delicas, bugles, seed beads, large plastic bead, silver wire   4" × 4" × 4"
Jill Cremer   Laguna Hills, California

I have wanted to do a fish form using beads for a number of years. The color and quality of the light that can be achieved through this medium works beautifully with underwater subjects.

See the Reef in Your Heart—Hold the Ocean in Your Hand
Frosted red whitehearts, pink and white coral, Caron embroidery thread   7" × 2½"
Linda Cronquist   Moscow, Idaho

Color, texture, and the overall integrity of the materials used are important to me. My materials can be pricey or inexpensive, but they must fit my mental image of what I want the piece to be. Creating is a very personal process—each piece I make holds a bit of myself.

World's Greatest Juggler—Working Mom of the 90's
Seed beads, delicas, plastic bead   4" × 5" × 1"
JoAnn Feher   Seattle, Washington

I am constantly amazed at what can be created with seed beads and thread. My beadwork is whimsical, intended to bring a smile to those who see it. **Working Mom** *is my first interactive piece—the wearer chooses what she will be juggling and where each piece will be placed.*

Juror's Choice

Bead Geode
Seed beads   3" × 2¾"
Anne Fletcher   Tucson, Arizona

Beads offer an incredible palette of color, shape, and texture with which to work. I find myself constantly thinking of new things to try. I like the freedom and excitement of starting with only the sketchiest of plans and letting the beads dictate the final outcome.

Bead Knitting
Seed beads, wooden beads 4" × 3½" × 3"
Anne Fletcher   Tucson, Arizona

Bead Soup

Seed beads, buttons, charms, wooden bowl, clay filling   4" × 2½"
Anne Fletcher   Tucson, Arizona

Juror's Choice

In Memory of Noah, April 19–July 13, 1996
Glass seed beads, metal beads, leather, vinyl, found objects, nylon thread   4" × 2½" × 3½"
Susan Etcoff Fraerman   Highland Park, Illinois

For many years, I equated fulfilling creative work with a cast of players, a stage, and an audience. Today I create images in reflective solitude surrounded by an array of glass beads. I create works that people want to touch—works that tell a story.

Juror's Choice

Memory Map: Gary's Tree
Seed beads   3" × 3"
Phyllis Fredendall-McIntyre   Hancock, Michigan

When my husband tells a story he often illustrates it with a small drawing—usually a map. These precious charts have found their way into my work. Saved for the retelling, these are maps of our conversations—shared memories stitched in glass.

Memory Map: Baraga Survey
Seed beads   4" × 4"
Phyllis Fredendall-McIntyre   Hancock, Michigan

Masquerade
Seed beads, fabric, stone 3½" × 3" × 3"
Valorie Harlow   Chanhassen, Minnesota

I created this piece to remind myself that people are infinitely more than the masks they present to the public.

Trouble in Paradise
Seed beads, fabric   4" × 4" × 4"
Valorie Harlow   Chanhassen, Minnesota

Belief in an unseen monster inspired this piece. I just haven't been able to capture the elusive creature eating the flowers in my garden.

Butterfly Beads
Sterling silver, enamel, copper, garnet 18" × ½"
Allison Johnson   De Kalb, Illinois

In learning various metalworking techniques, I've found bead forms to be a great "canvas" for experimentation. This necklace is a result of inquiry into casting hollow forms. Its lightweight nature supports the function of adornment.

Cuff-Links
Czech charlottes, Japanese beads   3⅜" × 1⅛"
Jacqueline Johnson   Yonkers, New York

This bracelet is the most recent expression of my ongoing fascination with beads and the seemingly limitless design possibilities in the making and joining of small repeating forms.

Private Eye
Seed beads, drops, glass eye-wash cup   3½" × 2"
Ella Johnson-Bentley   Juneau, Alaska

As soon as I saw the antique eye-wash cup, I knew what I wanted to make with it. Terry Pyles, wildlife artist and beadmaker from Ketchikan, Alaska, made the eyeball bead for me. I create beaded jewelry but like to make "whimsies" best.

Juror's Choice

Beware! Bee Wear
Seed beads, cotton thread, wire   4" × 4" × 4"
Laura Leonard   Minneapolis, Minnesota

No serious art from me. My pieces are story sculptures celebrating scenes from everyday life. This summer I had two bee stings in one week—so it was easy to decide on the subject matter when I asked myself "What would frighten me Up Close?" Gladys's expression and beehive hairdo carry through my fear and my humor.

Arterial Embrace
Seed beads, bugle beads   4" × 4" × 3"
Donna Lish   Clinton, New Jersey

My recent sculptures are a blend of the interaction of light and the illumination of pattern. I am fascinated by the linear progression inherent in beading. As beads are manipulated on the needle, variations naturally emerge, but still take on a rigid form.

Fiddleheads at Night
Beads, buttons, leather, wire, cotton floss   1¾" × ½"
Nor List   Durango, Colorado

My small pieces are very personal. On them I feel I can afford to be lavish and still keep my focus. Larger pieces tend to take longer because with so much space I get lost—so working small becomes a challenge, and from that challenge comes growth.

L.A. Egg
Seed beads, bugles   2" × 2" × 4"
Eleanor Lux   Eureka Springs, Arkansas

Beads allow me to express my ideas and feelings more easily than any other medium I've tried. There is the added excitement of watching as light falls on each bead and is absorbed by the bead, reflected off the bead, or passes through the bead.

Bird Vessel
Delicas   2" × 3¼"
Sue Maguire   Stevenage, Herts, United Kingdom

This piece is inspired by up-close investigations into Guatemalan textiles and architectural details on Saint Albans Cathedral in Hertfordshire. Next I plan on making a series of animal vessels.

Editor's Pick

Iris Coin Purse
Glass beads, plastic bead, tube, crochet thread   3½" × 3"
Yoshie Marubashi   New York, New York

Dear Heart
Delicas   3¼" × 3½"
Robin Matthews   Hollywood, California

This piece was inspired by Georgia O'Keeffe's painting, Bleeding Heart, *c. 1928.*

Seeing is Believing
Antique glass seed beads, magnifying glass, fabric   2½" × 3"
Carol Perrenoud   Wilsonville, Oregon

I enjoy weaving with the tiniest beads because of the resolution that can be achieved and the subtle gradation of colors. I grow heirloom perennial flowers and have always enjoyed the fashions and accessories of Edwardian and Victorian times. This is part of a series of beadworker's weaving accessories—or a beadworker's chatelaine.

Chessboard
Seed beads, antique beads   1" × 1" × ⅛"
Li Chien Raven   Evanston, Illinois

I enjoy creating work that has a playful nature—pieces that are familiar to the observer—and utilizing color to represent everyday objects.

Juror's Choice

Sink
Seed beads, fimo base   2½" × ½" × ½"
Li Chien Raven   Evanston, Illinois

Jealousy Maze
Seed beads, wooden bead   3½" × 3" × 3"
Ruth Marie Satterlee   Seattle, Washington

During 1998 I studied with NanC Meinhardt in a yearlong course exploring the theme of mazes. I am making a series of beaded beads expressing mazes I have encountered in life. My jealousies can appear silly to the outsider, but they will send me spinning off in many directions.

She Looked Different Up Close
Beads, wool felt   4" × 4"
Devony Smith   Madison, Wisconsin

Playing with the idea of "Up Close," I tried to express how our images and impressions of each other and the world change and vary with different levels of closeness.

Heart
Seed beads, velvet, wire, metallic threads   4" × 3¼"
Marcie Stone   San Diego, California

Working with a palette of beads and threads, I make spontaneous choices evolving into a biomorphic synthesis of color and textures. I am fascinated with the way the different beads play against each other and create jeweled encrustations. I am influenced by primitive art and organic forms.

Before the Millennium, USA
Charlotte seed beads, deer hide, metal belt buckle   3½" × 2⅝"
Mary Tafoya   Albuquerque, New Mexico

 This is Prophecy, the white buffalo calf born in Wisconsin, depicted with Hale-Bopp and the total lunar eclipse. I sat on my bed in the dark one evening, watching the comet out one window and the eclipse out the other, while my neighbors partied in the street. The gentle curve of the buckle somehow reminds me of looking through the porthole of a spaceship. The fence and the red, white, and blue define the scene as actual events in a certain time and space.

A Close Look at the Rare Female Sea Creature: The Vanemone
Seed beads   2" diameter
Judy Walker   Irvine, California

The Vanemone *is a humorous exploration of intimate femininity.*

Seed Bead Pod: Close to Bursting
Seed beads, teardrops, styrofoam ball wrapped in cotton   3" diameter
Judy Walker   Irvine, California

Seed Bead Pod: Close to Bursting *is my attempt to express the rich forms of bursting fertile life, using multi-layered textures, geometric patterns, rich colors, and shapes derived from nature.*

Baby Brownie
Beads, jewelry, camera   3½" × 3" × 3¼"
Kathy Wegman   Iowa City, Iowa

My husband and I are both collectors—we enjoy color and pattern. I collect ordinary objects and make them exciting with intense color and design.

Bird in Hand
Delicas, porcelain artist bead   1½" × 3"
Judi Wood   West Palm Beach, Florida

For me, creating art is as natural as breathing. My attraction to beads as an art form was an accident waiting to happen.

Index

Aubrey, Barbara 9
Bast, Joanne. 10
Baumann, Jo Ann 11, 12
Berkowitz, Bonnie 13
Bernhardt, Ingrid 14, 15, 16
Biagoli, Theresa 17
Bousquet-Smith, Bonnie. 18, 19
Breda, Bo 20
Crane, Marian 21, 22
Cremer, Jill. 23
Cronquist, Linda 24
Feher, JoAnn 25
Fletcher, Anne 26, 27, 28
Etcoff Fraerman, Susan 29
Fredendall-McIntyre, Phyllis . . . 30, 31
Harlow, Valorie 32, 33
Johnson, Allison 34
Johnson, Jacqueline 35

Johnson-Bentley, Ella 36
Leonard, Laura 37
Lish, Donna 38
List, Nor. 39
Lux, Eleanor. 40
Maquire, Sue 41
Marubashi, Yoshie. 42
Matthews, Robin. 43
Perrenoud, Carol. 44
Raven, Li Chien. 45, 46
Satterlee, Ruth Marie 47
Smith, Devony 48
Stone, Marcie 49
Tafoya, Mary 50
Walker, Judy 51, 52
Wegman, Kathy 53
Wood, Judi. 54